35 Burrito Recipes for Home

By: Kelly Johnson

Table of Contents

- Classic Beef Burrito
- Chicken and Rice Burrito
- Vegetarian Bean Burrito
- Breakfast Burrito with Eggs, Bacon, and Cheese
- Shrimp Burrito with Avocado Salsa
- Pulled Pork Burrito with BBQ Sauce
- Black Bean and Corn Burrito
- Steak and Cheese Burrito
- Sweet Potato and Black Bean Burrito
- Buffalo Chicken Burrito
- BBQ Beef Brisket Burrito
- Veggie Fajita Burrito
- Spicy Chipotle Chicken Burrito
- Hawaiian Pineapple Pork Burrito
- Tofu and Veggie Burrito
- Chorizo Breakfast Burrito
- Turkey and Cranberry Burrito
- Chili Verde Burrito with Pork
- Grilled Veggie Burrito with Hummus
- Teriyaki Chicken Burrito
- Southwest Chicken Burrito
- Carnitas Burrito with Salsa Verde
- Vegan Lentil Burrito
- Greek Gyro Burrito
- Cajun Shrimp Burrito
- Sriracha Beef Burrito
- Breakfast Sausage and Hash Brown Burrito
- Korean BBQ Beef Burrito
- Jackfruit Carnitas Burrito
- Thai Peanut Chicken Burrito
- Spinach and Mushroom Breakfast Burrito
- Hawaiian BBQ Chicken Burrito
- Bacon, Egg, and Cheese Breakfast Burrito
- Mediterranean Falafel Burrito
- Tex-Mex Beef Burrito Bowl

Classic Beef Burrito

Ingredients:

- 1 lb ground beef
- 1 small onion, diced
- 2 cloves garlic, minced
- 1 tablespoon olive oil
- 1 packet (1.25 oz) taco seasoning mix
- 1/4 cup water
- 1 cup cooked rice
- 1 can (15 oz) black beans, drained and rinsed
- 1 cup shredded cheddar cheese
- 8 large flour tortillas
- Salt and pepper to taste
- Optional toppings: shredded lettuce, diced tomatoes, salsa, sour cream, guacamole

Instructions:

Heat olive oil in a large skillet over medium heat. Add diced onion and minced garlic, sauté until softened, about 2-3 minutes.

Add ground beef to the skillet. Break it up with a spatula and cook until browned and no longer pink, about 5-7 minutes.

Drain excess fat from the skillet if necessary. Add taco seasoning mix and water to the beef mixture. Stir well to combine. Simmer for 2-3 minutes until the sauce thickens slightly. Season with salt and pepper to taste.

Warm the flour tortillas in a separate skillet or microwave according to package instructions to make them pliable.

Assemble the burritos: Place a spoonful of cooked rice in the center of each tortilla. Top with a spoonful of black beans and a portion of the seasoned beef mixture. Sprinkle shredded cheese over the filling.

Fold the sides of the tortilla over the filling, then roll it up tightly into a burrito.

Optional: If desired, lightly grill or toast the assembled burritos in a skillet to seal and crisp the edges.

Serve the beef burritos hot, with optional toppings such as shredded lettuce, diced tomatoes, salsa, sour cream, or guacamole on the side. Enjoy!

Chicken and Rice Burrito

Ingredients:

- 1 lb boneless, skinless chicken breasts, diced
- 1 cup white rice
- 1 tablespoon olive oil
- 1 small onion, diced
- 2 cloves garlic, minced
- 1 bell pepper, diced
- 1 teaspoon ground cumin
- 1 teaspoon chili powder
- Salt and pepper to taste
- 1 cup chicken broth
- 1 can (15 oz) black beans, drained and rinsed
- 1 cup shredded cheddar cheese
- 8 large flour tortillas
- Optional toppings: shredded lettuce, diced tomatoes, salsa, sour cream, guacamole

Instructions:

Cook the white rice according to package instructions. Set aside.

Heat olive oil in a large skillet over medium heat. Add diced onion, minced garlic, and diced bell pepper. Sauté until softened, about 3-4 minutes.

Add diced chicken to the skillet. Season with ground cumin, chili powder, salt, and pepper. Cook until the chicken is no longer pink, about 5-7 minutes.

Pour chicken broth into the skillet and bring to a simmer. Allow the chicken mixture to simmer until the liquid reduces slightly, about 5 minutes.

Add cooked rice and black beans to the skillet with the chicken mixture. Stir well to combine and heat through.

Warm the flour tortillas in a separate skillet or microwave according to package instructions to make them pliable.

Assemble the burritos: Place a spoonful of the chicken and rice mixture in the center of each tortilla. Sprinkle shredded cheese over the filling.

Fold the sides of the tortilla over the filling, then roll it up tightly into a burrito.

Optional: If desired, lightly grill or toast the assembled burritos in a skillet to seal and crisp the edges.

Serve the chicken and rice burritos hot, with optional toppings such as shredded lettuce, diced tomatoes, salsa, sour cream, or guacamole on the side. Enjoy!

Vegetarian Bean Burrito

Ingredients:

- 1 can (15 oz) black beans, drained and rinsed
- 1 can (15 oz) pinto beans, drained and rinsed
- 1 cup cooked rice
- 1 tablespoon olive oil
- 1 small onion, diced
- 2 cloves garlic, minced
- 1 bell pepper, diced
- 1 teaspoon ground cumin
- 1 teaspoon chili powder
- Salt and pepper to taste
- 1 cup shredded cheddar cheese
- 8 large flour tortillas
- Optional toppings: shredded lettuce, diced tomatoes, salsa, sour cream, guacamole

Instructions:

Heat olive oil in a large skillet over medium heat. Add diced onion, minced garlic, and diced bell pepper. Sauté until softened, about 3-4 minutes.

Add drained and rinsed black beans and pinto beans to the skillet. Season with ground cumin, chili powder, salt, and pepper. Stir well to combine and cook until heated through, about 5 minutes.

Stir in cooked rice until well combined with the bean mixture. Cook for an additional 2-3 minutes to heat through.

Warm the flour tortillas in a separate skillet or microwave according to package instructions to make them pliable.

Assemble the burritos: Place a spoonful of the bean and rice mixture in the center of each tortilla. Sprinkle shredded cheese over the filling.

Fold the sides of the tortilla over the filling, then roll it up tightly into a burrito.

Optional: If desired, lightly grill or toast the assembled burritos in a skillet to seal and crisp the edges.

Serve the vegetarian bean burritos hot, with optional toppings such as shredded lettuce, diced tomatoes, salsa, sour cream, or guacamole on the side. Enjoy!

Breakfast Burrito with Eggs, Bacon, and Cheese

Ingredients:

- 8 large eggs
- 8 slices of bacon
- 1 tablespoon butter or oil
- 1 cup shredded cheddar cheese
- 8 large flour tortillas
- Salt and pepper to taste
- Optional toppings: salsa, diced tomatoes, sliced avocado, sour cream, chopped green onions

Instructions:

Cook the bacon in a skillet over medium heat until crispy. Remove from the skillet and drain on paper towels. Once cooled, crumble the bacon into pieces.
In the same skillet, melt the butter over medium heat. Crack the eggs into the skillet and scramble them until cooked through. Season with salt and pepper to taste.
Warm the flour tortillas in a separate skillet or microwave according to package instructions to make them pliable.
Assemble the burritos: Place a portion of scrambled eggs in the center of each tortilla. Sprinkle with a portion of crumbled bacon and shredded cheddar cheese. Fold the sides of the tortilla over the filling, then roll it up tightly into a burrito.
Optional: If desired, lightly grill or toast the assembled burritos in a skillet to seal and crisp the edges.
Serve the breakfast burritos hot, with optional toppings such as salsa, diced tomatoes, sliced avocado, sour cream, or chopped green onions on the side.
Enjoy your delicious breakfast!

Shrimp Burrito with Avocado Salsa

Ingredients:

For the Shrimp:

- 1 lb large shrimp, peeled and deveined
- 1 tablespoon olive oil
- 1 teaspoon chili powder
- 1/2 teaspoon ground cumin
- Salt and pepper to taste

For the Avocado Salsa:

- 2 ripe avocados, diced
- 1 tomato, diced
- 1/4 cup red onion, finely chopped
- 1/4 cup fresh cilantro, chopped
- Juice of 1 lime
- Salt and pepper to taste

Additional Ingredients:

- 1 cup cooked rice
- 1 can (15 oz) black beans, drained and rinsed
- 1 cup shredded Monterey Jack cheese
- 8 large flour tortillas

Instructions:

In a bowl, toss the shrimp with olive oil, chili powder, cumin, salt, and pepper until evenly coated.

Heat a skillet over medium heat. Add the seasoned shrimp and cook until pink and cooked through, about 2-3 minutes per side. Remove from heat and set aside.

In a separate bowl, combine diced avocados, tomato, red onion, cilantro, lime juice, salt, and pepper to make the avocado salsa. Mix well and set aside.

Warm the flour tortillas in a separate skillet or microwave according to package instructions to make them pliable.

Assemble the burritos: Place a spoonful of cooked rice in the center of each tortilla. Top with a spoonful of black beans, a portion of cooked shrimp, and a spoonful of avocado salsa. Sprinkle shredded Monterey Jack cheese over the filling.

Fold the sides of the tortilla over the filling, then roll it up tightly into a burrito.

Optional: If desired, lightly grill or toast the assembled burritos in a skillet to seal and crisp the edges.

Serve the shrimp burritos hot, with extra avocado salsa on the side if desired. Enjoy your delicious meal!

Pulled Pork Burrito with BBQ Sauce

Ingredients:

For the Pulled Pork:

- 2 lbs pork shoulder or pork butt, trimmed of excess fat
- 1 tablespoon olive oil
- Salt and pepper to taste
- 1 cup barbecue sauce

For the Burrito:

- 1 cup cooked rice
- 1 can (15 oz) black beans, drained and rinsed
- 1 cup shredded cheddar cheese
- 8 large flour tortillas
- Optional toppings: diced tomatoes, diced red onion, shredded lettuce, sour cream, guacamole

Instructions:

Preheat the oven to 325°F (160°C).

Rub the pork shoulder with olive oil, salt, and pepper. Place it in a roasting pan or Dutch oven.

Cover the roasting pan or Dutch oven with aluminum foil and roast in the preheated oven for 3-4 hours, or until the pork is tender and easily shreds with a fork.

Remove the pork from the oven and let it cool slightly. Shred the pork using two forks, discarding any excess fat.

In a saucepan, heat the barbecue sauce over medium heat. Add the shredded pork to the sauce and stir to coat evenly. Cook for an additional 5-10 minutes, until the pork is heated through and absorbs some of the sauce.

Warm the flour tortillas in a separate skillet or microwave according to package instructions to make them pliable.

Assemble the burritos: Place a spoonful of cooked rice in the center of each tortilla. Top with a spoonful of black beans, a portion of pulled pork with barbecue sauce, and a sprinkle of shredded cheddar cheese.

Fold the sides of the tortilla over the filling, then roll it up tightly into a burrito.
Optional: If desired, lightly grill or toast the assembled burritos in a skillet to seal and crisp the edges.
Serve the pulled pork burritos hot, with optional toppings such as diced tomatoes, diced red onion, shredded lettuce, sour cream, or guacamole on the side. Enjoy your flavorful meal!

Steak and Cheese Burrito

Ingredients:

- 1 pound of steak (sirloin or flank steak works well), thinly sliced
- 1 onion, thinly sliced
- 1 bell pepper, thinly sliced
- 1 cup shredded cheese (cheddar, Monterey Jack, or your favorite cheese)
- 4 large flour tortillas
- Salt and pepper to taste
- Optional toppings: salsa, sour cream, guacamole, chopped cilantro

Instructions:

Season the thinly sliced steak with salt and pepper.
Heat a skillet over medium-high heat and add a little oil.
Add the steak slices to the skillet and cook until browned on both sides, about 3-4 minutes per side. Remove from the skillet and set aside.
In the same skillet, add a bit more oil if needed and add the sliced onions and bell peppers. Cook until they are softened and slightly caramelized, about 5-7 minutes.
Warm the flour tortillas in a separate skillet or microwave for a few seconds until they are pliable.
To assemble the burritos, lay out a tortilla and add a portion of the cooked steak slices to the center.
Top the steak with some of the cooked onions and bell peppers.
Sprinkle shredded cheese on top of the steak and vegetables.
Fold the sides of the tortilla over the filling, then roll it up tightly into a burrito.
Repeat with the remaining tortillas and filling ingredients.
If desired, you can heat the assembled burritos in a skillet over medium heat for a few minutes on each side to melt the cheese and crisp up the tortilla.
Serve the steak and cheese burritos with your favorite toppings such as salsa, sour cream, guacamole, or chopped cilantro.

Enjoy your delicious homemade steak and cheese burritos!

Sweet Potato and Black Bean Burrito

Ingredients:

- 2 medium sweet potatoes, peeled and diced
- 1 can (15 ounces) black beans, drained and rinsed
- 1 onion, diced
- 2 cloves garlic, minced
- 1 teaspoon ground cumin
- 1 teaspoon chili powder
- Salt and pepper to taste
- 4 large flour tortillas
- 1 cup shredded cheese (cheddar, Monterey Jack, or your favorite cheese)
- Optional toppings: salsa, sour cream, guacamole, chopped cilantro

Instructions:

Preheat your oven to 400°F (200°C).
Place the diced sweet potatoes on a baking sheet lined with parchment paper.
Drizzle with olive oil and sprinkle with salt and pepper. Toss to coat.
Roast the sweet potatoes in the preheated oven for 20-25 minutes, or until they are tender and lightly browned.
While the sweet potatoes are roasting, heat a little oil in a skillet over medium heat.
Add the diced onion to the skillet and cook until it becomes translucent, about 5 minutes.
Add the minced garlic to the skillet and cook for an additional minute.
Stir in the drained and rinsed black beans, ground cumin, chili powder, salt, and pepper. Cook for another 2-3 minutes until heated through.
Once the sweet potatoes are done roasting, add them to the skillet with the black bean mixture. Stir to combine and cook for another minute or two.
Warm the flour tortillas in a separate skillet or microwave for a few seconds until they are pliable.
To assemble the burritos, spoon some of the sweet potato and black bean mixture onto the center of each tortilla.
Sprinkle shredded cheese on top of the sweet potato and black bean mixture.
Fold the sides of the tortilla over the filling, then roll it up tightly into a burrito.
Repeat with the remaining tortillas and filling ingredients.

If desired, you can heat the assembled burritos in a skillet over medium heat for a few minutes on each side to melt the cheese and crisp up the tortilla.
Serve the sweet potato and black bean burritos with your favorite toppings such as salsa, sour cream, guacamole, or chopped cilantro.

Enjoy your delicious homemade sweet potato and black bean burritos!

Buffalo Chicken Burrito

Ingredients:

- 2 boneless, skinless chicken breasts
- 1/2 cup Buffalo sauce (store-bought or homemade)
- 1/4 cup ranch dressing or blue cheese dressing
- 1 cup cooked rice
- 1/2 cup shredded lettuce
- 1/4 cup diced tomatoes
- 1/4 cup diced red onion
- 1/4 cup diced celery
- 4 large flour tortillas
- 1 cup shredded cheese (cheddar, Monterey Jack, or your favorite cheese)
- Optional toppings: diced avocado, sliced green onions, chopped cilantro

Instructions:

Preheat your oven to 375°F (190°C).
Place the chicken breasts on a baking sheet lined with parchment paper. Season with salt and pepper.
Bake the chicken in the preheated oven for 20-25 minutes, or until cooked through. Remove from the oven and let it cool slightly.
Once the chicken is cool enough to handle, shred it using two forks or your fingers.
In a bowl, toss the shredded chicken with the Buffalo sauce until it is evenly coated.
In another bowl, mix together the cooked rice, ranch dressing, shredded lettuce, diced tomatoes, diced red onion, and diced celery.
Warm the flour tortillas in a separate skillet or microwave for a few seconds until they are pliable.
To assemble the burritos, spoon some of the rice and vegetable mixture onto the center of each tortilla.
Top the rice mixture with a portion of the Buffalo chicken.
Sprinkle shredded cheese on top of the chicken.
Fold the sides of the tortilla over the filling, then roll it up tightly into a burrito.
Repeat with the remaining tortillas and filling ingredients.

If desired, you can heat the assembled burritos in a skillet over medium heat for a few minutes on each side to melt the cheese and crisp up the tortilla.
Serve the Buffalo chicken burritos with your favorite toppings such as diced avocado, sliced green onions, or chopped cilantro.

Enjoy your flavorful homemade Buffalo chicken burritos!

BBQ Beef Brisket Burrito

Ingredients:

- 1 pound beef brisket
- Salt and pepper to taste
- 1 cup BBQ sauce (your favorite variety)
- 1 onion, sliced
- 1 bell pepper, sliced
- 4 large flour tortillas
- 1 cup cooked rice
- 1 cup shredded cheese (cheddar, Monterey Jack, or your favorite cheese)
- Optional toppings: diced tomatoes, diced red onion, sliced avocado, chopped cilantro

Instructions:

Preheat your oven to 300°F (150°C).
Season the beef brisket generously with salt and pepper.
Place the seasoned brisket in a roasting pan and cover it with foil.
Roast the brisket in the preheated oven for about 4-5 hours, or until it is tender and easily shreds with a fork.
Once the brisket is cooked, shred it using two forks or your fingers.
In a skillet over medium heat, sauté the sliced onion and bell pepper until they are softened and lightly caramelized, about 5-7 minutes.
Add the shredded beef brisket to the skillet along with the BBQ sauce. Stir to combine and cook for another 2-3 minutes until heated through.
Warm the flour tortillas in a separate skillet or microwave for a few seconds until they are pliable.
To assemble the burritos, spoon some of the cooked rice onto the center of each tortilla.
Top the rice with a portion of the BBQ beef brisket mixture.
Sprinkle shredded cheese on top of the brisket.
Add any optional toppings you desire, such as diced tomatoes, diced red onion, sliced avocado, or chopped cilantro.
Fold the sides of the tortilla over the filling, then roll it up tightly into a burrito.
Repeat with the remaining tortillas and filling ingredients.
If desired, you can heat the assembled burritos in a skillet over medium heat for a few minutes on each side to melt the cheese and crisp up the tortilla.
Serve the BBQ beef brisket burritos hot, and enjoy the delicious flavors!

This recipe will surely satisfy any BBQ lover's cravings!

Veggie Fajita Burrito

Ingredients:

- 2 bell peppers (any color), thinly sliced
- 1 onion, thinly sliced
- 2 cloves garlic, minced
- 1 tablespoon olive oil
- 1 teaspoon ground cumin
- 1 teaspoon chili powder
- Salt and pepper to taste
- 1 cup cooked rice
- 1 can (15 ounces) black beans, drained and rinsed
- 4 large flour tortillas
- 1 cup shredded cheese (cheddar, Monterey Jack, or your favorite cheese)
- Optional toppings: salsa, sour cream, guacamole, chopped cilantro

Instructions:

Heat the olive oil in a skillet over medium-high heat.
Add the sliced bell peppers and onion to the skillet. Cook, stirring occasionally, until the vegetables are softened and slightly charred, about 8-10 minutes.
Add the minced garlic, ground cumin, chili powder, salt, and pepper to the skillet with the vegetables. Cook for another minute until fragrant.
Stir in the cooked rice and black beans. Cook for an additional 2-3 minutes until heated through.
Warm the flour tortillas in a separate skillet or microwave for a few seconds until they are pliable.
To assemble the burritos, spoon some of the vegetable and rice mixture onto the center of each tortilla.
Sprinkle shredded cheese on top of the vegetable and rice mixture.
Add any optional toppings you desire, such as salsa, sour cream, guacamole, or chopped cilantro.
Fold the sides of the tortilla over the filling, then roll it up tightly into a burrito.
Repeat with the remaining tortillas and filling ingredients.
If desired, you can heat the assembled burritos in a skillet over medium heat for a few minutes on each side to melt the cheese and crisp up the tortilla.
Serve the veggie fajita burritos hot, and enjoy the delicious and nutritious flavors!

This veggie fajita burrito is packed with colorful vegetables, protein-rich black beans, and flavorful spices, making it a satisfying and healthy meal option.

Spicy Chipotle Chicken Burrito

Ingredients:

- 2 boneless, skinless chicken breasts
- Salt and pepper to taste
- 2 chipotle peppers in adobo sauce, minced
- 2 tablespoons adobo sauce (from the can of chipotle peppers)
- 2 cloves garlic, minced
- 1 teaspoon ground cumin
- 1 teaspoon chili powder
- 1 tablespoon lime juice
- 2 tablespoons olive oil
- 1 onion, diced
- 1 bell pepper, diced
- 1 cup cooked rice
- 1 can (15 ounces) black beans, drained and rinsed
- 4 large flour tortillas
- 1 cup shredded cheese (cheddar, Monterey Jack, or your favorite cheese)
- Optional toppings: diced tomatoes, diced red onion, sliced avocado, chopped cilantro, sour cream

Instructions:

Season the chicken breasts with salt and pepper on both sides.
In a bowl, combine the minced chipotle peppers, adobo sauce, minced garlic, ground cumin, chili powder, and lime juice. Mix well to form a marinade.
Place the chicken breasts in the marinade and coat them evenly. Let them marinate for at least 30 minutes, or overnight in the refrigerator for maximum flavor.
Heat 1 tablespoon of olive oil in a skillet over medium-high heat. Add the marinated chicken breasts and cook until they are browned and cooked through, about 6-7 minutes per side. Once cooked, remove them from the skillet and let them rest for a few minutes before slicing them thinly.
In the same skillet, heat the remaining tablespoon of olive oil over medium heat. Add the diced onion and bell pepper, and cook until they are softened, about 5-6 minutes.
Add the cooked rice and black beans to the skillet with the onion and bell pepper. Stir to combine and cook for another 2-3 minutes until heated through.

Warm the flour tortillas in a separate skillet or microwave for a few seconds until they are pliable.
To assemble the burritos, spoon some of the rice and vegetable mixture onto the center of each tortilla.
Top the rice mixture with slices of the chipotle chicken.
Sprinkle shredded cheese on top of the chicken.
Add any optional toppings you desire, such as diced tomatoes, diced red onion, sliced avocado, chopped cilantro, or sour cream.
Fold the sides of the tortilla over the filling, then roll it up tightly into a burrito.
Repeat with the remaining tortillas and filling ingredients.
If desired, you can heat the assembled burritos in a skillet over medium heat for a few minutes on each side to melt the cheese and crisp up the tortilla.
Serve the spicy chipotle chicken burritos hot, and enjoy the delicious and fiery flavors!

This spicy chipotle chicken burrito is perfect for those who crave a little heat in their meals. Adjust the amount of chipotle peppers to suit your spice preference.

Hawaiian Pineapple Pork Burrito

Ingredients:

- 1 pound pork shoulder or pork tenderloin, thinly sliced
- Salt and pepper to taste
- 1 cup pineapple chunks (fresh or canned)
- 1/2 cup BBQ sauce (your favorite variety)
- 1 tablespoon soy sauce
- 1 tablespoon brown sugar
- 1 tablespoon olive oil
- 1 onion, thinly sliced
- 1 bell pepper, thinly sliced
- 1 cup cooked rice
- 4 large flour tortillas
- 1 cup shredded cheese (cheddar, Monterey Jack, or your favorite cheese)
- Optional toppings: diced tomatoes, diced red onion, sliced avocado, chopped cilantro

Instructions:

Season the thinly sliced pork with salt and pepper.
In a bowl, combine the BBQ sauce, soy sauce, and brown sugar. Mix well to create the marinade.
Add the sliced pork to the marinade and toss to coat. Let it marinate for at least 30 minutes, or overnight in the refrigerator for maximum flavor.
Heat the olive oil in a skillet over medium-high heat. Add the marinated pork slices and cook until they are browned and cooked through, about 5-6 minutes per side. Once cooked, remove them from the skillet and set aside.
In the same skillet, add the thinly sliced onion and bell pepper. Cook until they are softened and slightly caramelized, about 5-6 minutes.
Add the cooked rice and pineapple chunks to the skillet with the onion and bell pepper. Stir to combine and cook for another 2-3 minutes until heated through.
Warm the flour tortillas in a separate skillet or microwave for a few seconds until they are pliable.
To assemble the burritos, spoon some of the rice and pineapple mixture onto the center of each tortilla.
Top the rice mixture with slices of the cooked pork.
Sprinkle shredded cheese on top of the pork.

Add any optional toppings you desire, such as diced tomatoes, diced red onion, sliced avocado, or chopped cilantro.
Fold the sides of the tortilla over the filling, then roll it up tightly into a burrito.
Repeat with the remaining tortillas and filling ingredients.
If desired, you can heat the assembled burritos in a skillet over medium heat for a few minutes on each side to melt the cheese and crisp up the tortilla.
Serve the Hawaiian pineapple pork burritos hot, and enjoy the delicious tropical flavors!

This Hawaiian-inspired burrito combines the sweetness of pineapple with savory pork and tangy BBQ sauce, creating a delightful taste of the islands in every bite.

Tofu and Veggie Burrito

Ingredients:

- 1 block (14-16 ounces) firm tofu, pressed and cubed
- 2 tablespoons soy sauce
- 1 tablespoon lime juice
- 1 teaspoon ground cumin
- 1 teaspoon chili powder
- 1/2 teaspoon garlic powder
- Salt and pepper to taste
- 1 tablespoon olive oil
- 1 onion, diced
- 1 bell pepper, diced
- 2 cups sliced mushrooms
- 2 cups spinach or kale leaves, chopped
- 1 cup cooked rice
- 1 can (15 ounces) black beans, drained and rinsed
- 4 large flour tortillas
- 1 cup shredded cheese (cheddar, Monterey Jack, or your favorite cheese)
- Optional toppings: salsa, sour cream, guacamole, chopped cilantro

Instructions:

In a bowl, combine the cubed tofu, soy sauce, lime juice, ground cumin, chili powder, garlic powder, salt, and pepper. Toss to coat the tofu evenly in the marinade. Let it marinate for at least 15-20 minutes.

Heat the olive oil in a skillet over medium-high heat. Add the marinated tofu cubes to the skillet and cook until they are golden brown and slightly crispy on all sides, about 5-7 minutes. Once cooked, remove them from the skillet and set aside.

In the same skillet, add the diced onion, bell pepper, and sliced mushrooms. Cook until the vegetables are softened and lightly browned, about 5-7 minutes.

Add the chopped spinach or kale to the skillet and cook until wilted, about 2-3 minutes.

Stir in the cooked rice and black beans. Cook for another 2-3 minutes until heated through.

Warm the flour tortillas in a separate skillet or microwave for a few seconds until they are pliable.
To assemble the burritos, spoon some of the tofu and vegetable mixture onto the center of each tortilla.
Sprinkle shredded cheese on top of the tofu and vegetable mixture.
Add any optional toppings you desire, such as salsa, sour cream, guacamole, or chopped cilantro.
Fold the sides of the tortilla over the filling, then roll it up tightly into a burrito.
Repeat with the remaining tortillas and filling ingredients.
If desired, you can heat the assembled burritos in a skillet over medium heat for a few minutes on each side to melt the cheese and crisp up the tortilla.
Serve the tofu and veggie burritos hot, and enjoy the flavorful and nutritious meal!

This tofu and veggie burrito is packed with protein, fiber, and vitamins, making it a satisfying and wholesome option for lunch or dinner. Feel free to customize the vegetables and toppings according to your preferences.

Chorizo Breakfast Burrito

Ingredients:

- 8 ounces chorizo sausage, casing removed
- 6 large eggs
- Salt and pepper to taste
- 1 tablespoon olive oil
- 1 small onion, diced
- 1 bell pepper, diced
- 1 jalapeño pepper, seeded and diced (optional, for extra heat)
- 1 cup shredded cheese (cheddar, Monterey Jack, or your favorite cheese)
- 4 large flour tortillas
- Optional toppings: salsa, diced avocado, sour cream, chopped cilantro

Instructions:

Heat a skillet over medium-high heat. Add the chorizo sausage, breaking it up with a spatula as it cooks. Cook until the chorizo is browned and cooked through, about 5-7 minutes. Once cooked, remove the chorizo from the skillet and set it aside.

In a bowl, whisk together the eggs with salt and pepper to taste.

Heat the olive oil in the same skillet over medium heat. Add the diced onion, bell pepper, and jalapeño pepper (if using). Cook until the vegetables are softened, about 5-6 minutes.

Pour the whisked eggs into the skillet with the cooked vegetables. Cook, stirring occasionally, until the eggs are scrambled and cooked to your desired consistency.

Return the cooked chorizo to the skillet with the scrambled eggs. Stir to combine and heat through for another minute.

Warm the flour tortillas in a separate skillet or microwave for a few seconds until they are pliable.

To assemble the burritos, spoon some of the chorizo and egg mixture onto the center of each tortilla.

Sprinkle shredded cheese on top of the chorizo and eggs.

Add any optional toppings you desire, such as salsa, diced avocado, sour cream, or chopped cilantro.

Fold the sides of the tortilla over the filling, then roll it up tightly into a burrito.

Repeat with the remaining tortillas and filling ingredients.

If desired, you can heat the assembled burritos in a skillet over medium heat for a few minutes on each side to melt the cheese and crisp up the tortilla.

Serve the chorizo breakfast burritos hot, and enjoy the flavorful and satisfying breakfast!

This chorizo breakfast burrito is hearty, flavorful, and perfect for starting your day off right. Feel free to customize the recipe with your favorite breakfast ingredients and toppings.

Turkey and Cranberry Burrito

Ingredients:

- 2 cups cooked turkey, shredded or sliced
- 1/2 cup cranberry sauce (homemade or store-bought)
- 1 cup cooked rice
- 1/2 cup stuffing (optional)
- 4 large flour tortillas
- 1 cup shredded cheese (cheddar, Monterey Jack, or your favorite cheese)
- Optional toppings: diced avocado, sour cream, chopped green onions, chopped cilantro

Instructions:

Preheat your oven to 350°F (175°C).
In a bowl, mix together the cooked turkey and cranberry sauce until the turkey is evenly coated.
Warm the cooked rice and stuffing (if using) in the microwave or on the stove.
Warm the flour tortillas in a skillet or microwave for a few seconds until they are pliable.
To assemble the burritos, lay out a tortilla and add a portion of the cooked rice to the center.
Add a layer of the cranberry turkey mixture on top of the rice.
If using stuffing, add a spoonful of stuffing on top of the turkey mixture.
Sprinkle shredded cheese on top of the filling.
Add any optional toppings you desire, such as diced avocado, sour cream, chopped green onions, or chopped cilantro.
Fold the sides of the tortilla over the filling, then roll it up tightly into a burrito.
Repeat with the remaining tortillas and filling ingredients.
Place the assembled burritos on a baking sheet lined with parchment paper.
Bake in the preheated oven for 10-15 minutes, or until the cheese is melted and the burritos are heated through.
Serve the turkey and cranberry burritos hot, and enjoy the festive flavors!

This turkey and cranberry burrito is a delightful way to enjoy the flavors of Thanksgiving in a new and creative way. Feel free to customize the recipe with your favorite Thanksgiving leftovers and toppings.

Chili Verde Burrito with Pork

Ingredients:

- 1 pound pork shoulder, cut into cubes
- Salt and pepper to taste
- 2 tablespoons olive oil
- 1 onion, chopped
- 3 cloves garlic, minced
- 2 cans (4 ounces each) diced green chilies
- 1 cup salsa verde (green salsa)
- 1 cup chicken broth
- 1 teaspoon ground cumin
- 1 teaspoon dried oregano
- 1/2 teaspoon chili powder (optional, for extra heat)
- 4 large flour tortillas
- 1 cup cooked rice
- 1 cup shredded cheese (cheddar, Monterey Jack, or your favorite cheese)
- Optional toppings: sour cream, diced avocado, chopped cilantro, diced tomatoes

Instructions:

Season the pork cubes with salt and pepper.
Heat the olive oil in a large skillet or Dutch oven over medium-high heat. Add the pork cubes and cook until browned on all sides, about 5-7 minutes. Remove the pork from the skillet and set aside.
In the same skillet, add the chopped onion and cook until softened, about 5 minutes. Add the minced garlic and cook for an additional minute.
Return the browned pork to the skillet. Add the diced green chilies, salsa verde, chicken broth, ground cumin, dried oregano, and chili powder (if using). Stir to combine.
Bring the mixture to a simmer, then reduce the heat to low. Cover and let it simmer for 1 to 1.5 hours, stirring occasionally, until the pork is tender and the flavors have melded together.
Once the pork is tender, preheat your oven to 350°F (175°C).
Warm the flour tortillas in the microwave or in a skillet for a few seconds until they are pliable.

To assemble the burritos, spoon some of the pork chili verde mixture onto the center of each tortilla.

Add a spoonful of cooked rice on top of the pork mixture.

Sprinkle shredded cheese on top of the rice.

Add any optional toppings you desire, such as sour cream, diced avocado, chopped cilantro, or diced tomatoes.

Fold the sides of the tortilla over the filling, then roll it up tightly into a burrito.

Place the assembled burritos on a baking sheet lined with parchment paper.

Bake in the preheated oven for 10-15 minutes, or until the cheese is melted and the burritos are heated through.

Serve the Chili Verde Burritos with Pork hot, and enjoy the delicious flavors!

This Chili Verde Burrito with Pork is packed with tender pork in a flavorful green chili sauce, making it a satisfying and comforting meal option. Feel free to adjust the level of spice to your preference by adding more or less chili powder.

Grilled Veggie Burrito with Hummus

Ingredients:

- 2 large flour tortillas
- 1 cup hummus (store-bought or homemade)
- 1 zucchini, sliced lengthwise
- 1 yellow squash, sliced lengthwise
- 1 red bell pepper, sliced into strips
- 1 yellow bell pepper, sliced into strips
- 1 red onion, sliced into rings
- 1 cup cherry tomatoes
- 2 tablespoons olive oil
- Salt and pepper to taste
- Optional toppings: crumbled feta cheese, chopped fresh parsley, sliced black olives

Instructions:

Preheat your grill to medium-high heat.
In a large bowl, toss the sliced zucchini, yellow squash, bell peppers, red onion, and cherry tomatoes with olive oil, salt, and pepper until evenly coated.
Place the vegetables on the preheated grill. Cook for 5-7 minutes, flipping halfway through, until they are tender and lightly charred.
Remove the grilled vegetables from the grill and set aside.
Warm the flour tortillas on the grill for about 30 seconds on each side, until they are pliable.
To assemble the burritos, spread a layer of hummus onto each tortilla.
Place a portion of the grilled vegetables onto the center of each tortilla.
If desired, sprinkle crumbled feta cheese, chopped fresh parsley, and sliced black olives on top of the grilled vegetables.
Fold the sides of the tortilla over the filling, then roll it up tightly into a burrito.
Repeat with the remaining tortilla and filling ingredients.
If desired, you can heat the assembled burritos on the grill for a few minutes on each side to warm them up and melt the cheese.
Serve the Grilled Veggie Burritos with Hummus hot, and enjoy the delicious and nutritious meal!

These Grilled Veggie Burritos with Hummus are packed with flavorful grilled vegetables and creamy hummus, making them a satisfying and healthy option for lunch or dinner. Feel free to customize the recipe with your favorite vegetables and toppings.

Teriyaki Chicken Burrito

Ingredients:

- 2 boneless, skinless chicken breasts, thinly sliced
- 1/2 cup teriyaki sauce (store-bought or homemade)
- 1 tablespoon soy sauce
- 1 tablespoon honey
- 1 tablespoon olive oil
- 1 onion, thinly sliced
- 1 bell pepper, thinly sliced
- 1 cup cooked rice
- 4 large flour tortillas
- 1 cup shredded cheese (cheddar, Monterey Jack, or your favorite cheese)
- Optional toppings: sliced avocado, chopped green onions, sesame seeds

Instructions:

In a bowl, combine the teriyaki sauce, soy sauce, and honey. Mix well to create the marinade.

Add the thinly sliced chicken breasts to the marinade and toss to coat. Let them marinate for at least 30 minutes, or overnight in the refrigerator for maximum flavor.

Heat the olive oil in a skillet over medium-high heat. Add the marinated chicken slices to the skillet and cook until they are browned and cooked through, about 5-7 minutes per side. Once cooked, remove them from the skillet and set aside.

In the same skillet, add the thinly sliced onion and bell pepper. Cook until they are softened and lightly caramelized, about 5-7 minutes.

Return the cooked chicken to the skillet with the onions and bell peppers. Stir to combine and heat through for another minute.

Warm the flour tortillas in a separate skillet or microwave for a few seconds until they are pliable.

To assemble the burritos, spoon some of the cooked rice onto the center of each tortilla.

Top the rice with a portion of the teriyaki chicken mixture.

Sprinkle shredded cheese on top of the chicken.

Add any optional toppings you desire, such as sliced avocado, chopped green onions, or sesame seeds.

Fold the sides of the tortilla over the filling, then roll it up tightly into a burrito. Repeat with the remaining tortillas and filling ingredients.

If desired, you can heat the assembled burritos in a skillet over medium heat for a few minutes on each side to melt the cheese and crisp up the tortilla.

Serve the Teriyaki Chicken Burritos hot, and enjoy the delicious Asian-inspired flavors!

These Teriyaki Chicken Burritos are packed with savory teriyaki chicken, colorful vegetables, and fluffy rice, making them a flavorful and satisfying meal option. Feel free to customize the recipe with your favorite vegetables and toppings.

Southwest Chicken Burrito

Ingredients:

- 2 boneless, skinless chicken breasts, diced
- 1 tablespoon olive oil
- 1 onion, diced
- 1 bell pepper, diced
- 1 can (15 ounces) black beans, drained and rinsed
- 1 cup corn kernels (fresh, frozen, or canned)
- 1 teaspoon ground cumin
- 1 teaspoon chili powder
- Salt and pepper to taste
- 1 cup cooked rice
- 4 large flour tortillas
- 1 cup shredded cheese (cheddar, Monterey Jack, or your favorite cheese)
- Optional toppings: diced tomatoes, diced avocado, chopped cilantro, sour cream, salsa

Instructions:

Heat the olive oil in a skillet over medium-high heat. Add the diced chicken breasts to the skillet and cook until they are browned and cooked through, about 5-7 minutes. Once cooked, remove them from the skillet and set aside.
In the same skillet, add the diced onion and bell pepper. Cook until they are softened and lightly caramelized, about 5-7 minutes.
Add the drained and rinsed black beans, corn kernels, ground cumin, and chili powder to the skillet with the onions and bell peppers. Stir to combine and cook for another 2-3 minutes until heated through. Season with salt and pepper to taste.
Warm the flour tortillas in a separate skillet or microwave for a few seconds until they are pliable.
To assemble the burritos, spoon some of the cooked rice onto the center of each tortilla.
Top the rice with a portion of the chicken mixture.
Sprinkle shredded cheese on top of the chicken mixture.
Add any optional toppings you desire, such as diced tomatoes, diced avocado, chopped cilantro, sour cream, or salsa.

Fold the sides of the tortilla over the filling, then roll it up tightly into a burrito. Repeat with the remaining tortillas and filling ingredients.

If desired, you can heat the assembled burritos in a skillet over medium heat for a few minutes on each side to melt the cheese and crisp up the tortilla.

Serve the Southwest Chicken Burritos hot, and enjoy the flavorful and satisfying meal!

These Southwest Chicken Burritos are packed with protein, fiber, and bold flavors, making them a delicious and nutritious meal option. Feel free to customize the recipe with your favorite toppings and add-ons.

Carnitas Burrito with Salsa Verde

Ingredients:

For the Carnitas:

- 2 pounds pork shoulder, cut into large chunks
- 1 onion, quartered
- 4 cloves garlic, crushed
- 1 teaspoon ground cumin
- 1 teaspoon dried oregano
- 1 teaspoon salt
- 1/2 teaspoon black pepper
- 1 tablespoon olive oil
- 1 cup chicken broth

For the Salsa Verde:

- 6 tomatillos, husked and washed
- 1 jalapeño pepper, stemmed (remove seeds for milder salsa)
- 1/2 onion, chopped
- 2 cloves garlic
- 1/4 cup fresh cilantro leaves
- Juice of 1 lime
- Salt to taste

For the Burrito:

- 4 large flour tortillas
- 1 cup cooked rice
- 1 cup black beans, drained and rinsed
- 1 cup shredded cheese (cheddar, Monterey Jack, or your favorite cheese)
- Optional toppings: diced avocado, sour cream, chopped cilantro, lime wedges

Instructions:

Preheat your oven to 325°F (165°C).
To make the carnitas, season the pork shoulder chunks with ground cumin, dried oregano, salt, and black pepper.

Heat olive oil in a large oven-safe pot or Dutch oven over medium-high heat. Brown the pork shoulder chunks on all sides, about 3-4 minutes per side. Remove the pork from the pot and set aside.

In the same pot, add quartered onion and crushed garlic cloves. Sauté until aromatic, about 2 minutes.

Return the browned pork shoulder to the pot. Add chicken broth to cover the meat.

Cover the pot and transfer it to the preheated oven. Cook for 2 to 2.5 hours, or until the pork is tender and easily shreds with a fork.

While the pork is cooking, make the salsa verde. In a medium saucepan, combine the tomatillos, jalapeño pepper, chopped onion, and garlic cloves. Cover with water and bring to a boil. Reduce heat and simmer for 10-15 minutes, or until the tomatillos are soft.

Drain the cooked vegetables and transfer them to a blender. Add fresh cilantro leaves, lime juice, and salt to taste. Blend until smooth. Adjust seasoning if needed.

Once the pork is done cooking, remove it from the oven and shred it using two forks.

To assemble the burritos, warm the flour tortillas in the microwave or on a skillet. Place a portion of cooked rice, shredded carnitas, black beans, and shredded cheese on each tortilla.

Drizzle salsa verde over the filling.

Add any optional toppings you desire, such as diced avocado, sour cream, chopped cilantro, or lime wedges.

Fold the sides of the tortilla over the filling, then roll it up tightly into a burrito.

Serve the Carnitas Burrito with Salsa Verde hot, and enjoy the delicious flavors!

This Carnitas Burrito with Salsa Verde is packed with tender, flavorful pork, tangy salsa verde, and other delicious toppings, making it a satisfying meal option for any occasion. Feel free to customize the recipe with your favorite burrito fillings and toppings.

Vegan Lentil Burrito

Ingredients:

For the Lentil Filling:

- 1 cup dried lentils
- 3 cups vegetable broth or water
- 1 tablespoon olive oil
- 1 onion, diced
- 2 cloves garlic, minced
- 1 bell pepper, diced
- 1 teaspoon ground cumin
- 1 teaspoon chili powder
- 1/2 teaspoon paprika
- Salt and pepper to taste

For the Burrito:

- 4 large flour tortillas
- 1 cup cooked rice
- 1 cup canned black beans, drained and rinsed
- 1 cup corn kernels (fresh, frozen, or canned)
- 1 avocado, sliced
- 1/2 cup salsa (store-bought or homemade)
- Optional toppings: diced tomatoes, shredded lettuce, chopped cilantro, vegan cheese, lime wedges

Instructions:

Rinse the lentils under cold water and drain.

In a medium saucepan, combine the lentils and vegetable broth or water. Bring to a boil, then reduce heat to low and simmer for about 20-25 minutes, or until the lentils are tender. Drain any excess liquid and set aside.

In a large skillet, heat olive oil over medium heat. Add diced onion and cook until translucent, about 3-4 minutes. Add minced garlic and diced bell pepper, and cook for another 2-3 minutes until softened.

Add cooked lentils to the skillet with the sautéed vegetables. Stir in ground cumin, chili powder, paprika, salt, and pepper. Cook for an additional 2-3 minutes to allow the flavors to meld together. Remove from heat.

Warm the flour tortillas in the microwave or on a skillet.

To assemble the burritos, place a portion of cooked rice, lentil filling, black beans, corn kernels, sliced avocado, and salsa onto each tortilla.

Add any optional toppings you desire, such as diced tomatoes, shredded lettuce, chopped cilantro, vegan cheese, or a squeeze of lime juice.

Fold the sides of the tortilla over the filling, then roll it up tightly into a burrito. Repeat with the remaining tortillas and filling ingredients.

Serve the Vegan Lentil Burritos immediately, and enjoy the delicious and nutritious meal!

These Vegan Lentil Burritos are packed with protein, fiber, and wholesome ingredients, making them a satisfying and flavorful meal option for vegans and non-vegans alike. Feel free to customize the recipe with your favorite burrito fillings and toppings.

Greek Gyro Burrito

Ingredients:

For the Gyro Meat:

- 1 pound ground lamb or beef (or a combination)
- 1 onion, grated
- 2 cloves garlic, minced
- 1 tablespoon dried oregano
- 1 teaspoon ground cumin
- 1 teaspoon paprika
- Salt and pepper to taste

For the Tzatziki Sauce:

- 1 cup Greek yogurt
- 1/2 cucumber, grated and squeezed to remove excess moisture
- 1 clove garlic, minced
- 1 tablespoon lemon juice
- 1 tablespoon chopped fresh dill (or 1 teaspoon dried dill)
- Salt and pepper to taste

For the Burrito:

- 4 large flour tortillas
- 1 cup cooked rice
- 1 cup diced tomatoes
- 1 cup diced cucumbers
- 1/2 cup crumbled feta cheese
- Optional toppings: chopped red onion, sliced black olives, chopped fresh parsley, lemon wedges

Instructions:

Preheat your oven to 375°F (190°C).

In a large mixing bowl, combine the ground lamb or beef with grated onion, minced garlic, dried oregano, ground cumin, paprika, salt, and pepper. Mix well until all the ingredients are evenly distributed.

Shape the meat mixture into small logs or patties, resembling traditional gyro meat.

Place the gyro meat on a baking sheet lined with parchment paper. Bake in the preheated oven for 20-25 minutes, or until the meat is cooked through and slightly browned.

While the gyro meat is baking, prepare the tzatziki sauce. In a medium bowl, combine Greek yogurt, grated cucumber, minced garlic, lemon juice, chopped fresh dill, salt, and pepper. Mix well to combine. Adjust seasoning to taste.

Warm the flour tortillas in the microwave or on a skillet.

To assemble the burritos, spread a layer of cooked rice onto each tortilla.

Add a portion of diced tomatoes, diced cucumbers, and crumbled feta cheese on top of the rice.

Place a few pieces of baked gyro meat on top of the vegetables and cheese.

Drizzle tzatziki sauce over the filling.

Add any optional toppings you desire, such as chopped red onion, sliced black olives, chopped fresh parsley, or a squeeze of lemon juice.

Fold the sides of the tortilla over the filling, then roll it up tightly into a burrito.

Serve the Greek Gyro Burritos immediately, and enjoy the delicious Mediterranean flavors!

These Greek Gyro Burritos are packed with savory gyro meat, fresh vegetables, tangy tzatziki sauce, and creamy feta cheese, making them a flavorful and satisfying meal option. Feel free to customize the recipe with your favorite gyro fillings and toppings.

Cajun Shrimp Burrito

Ingredients:

For the Cajun Shrimp:

- 1 pound large shrimp, peeled and deveined
- 2 tablespoons Cajun seasoning
- 2 tablespoons olive oil
- Juice of 1 lime

For the Burrito:

- 4 large flour tortillas
- 1 cup cooked rice
- 1 cup black beans, drained and rinsed
- 1 cup diced tomatoes
- 1 cup diced bell peppers (any color)
- 1/2 cup diced red onion
- 1 avocado, sliced
- 1/4 cup chopped fresh cilantro
- Optional toppings: shredded cheese, sour cream, salsa, hot sauce

Instructions:

In a bowl, toss the peeled and deveined shrimp with Cajun seasoning, olive oil, and lime juice until evenly coated. Let it marinate for about 15 minutes.

Heat a large skillet over medium-high heat. Add the marinated shrimp to the skillet and cook for 2-3 minutes per side, or until they are pink and cooked through. Remove from heat and set aside.

Warm the flour tortillas in the microwave or on a skillet.

To assemble the burritos, place a portion of cooked rice, black beans, diced tomatoes, diced bell peppers, and diced red onion onto each tortilla.

Add a few cooked Cajun shrimp to each burrito.

Top with sliced avocado and chopped fresh cilantro.

Add any optional toppings you desire, such as shredded cheese, sour cream, salsa, or hot sauce.

Fold the sides of the tortilla over the filling, then roll it up tightly into a burrito. Serve the Cajun Shrimp Burritos immediately, and enjoy the spicy and flavorful meal!

These Cajun Shrimp Burritos are packed with tender shrimp seasoned with Cajun spices, along with rice, beans, vegetables, and creamy avocado, making them a delicious and satisfying meal option. Feel free to customize the recipe with your favorite burrito fillings and toppings. Enjoy!

Sriracha Beef Burrito

Ingredients:

For the Sriracha Beef:

- 1 pound ground beef
- 2 tablespoons Sriracha sauce (adjust to taste)
- 2 tablespoons soy sauce
- 2 cloves garlic, minced
- 1 tablespoon brown sugar
- 1 tablespoon sesame oil
- Salt and pepper to taste

For the Burrito:

- 4 large flour tortillas
- 1 cup cooked rice
- 1 cup black beans, drained and rinsed
- 1 cup diced tomatoes
- 1 cup shredded lettuce
- 1 avocado, sliced
- 1/4 cup chopped green onions
- Optional toppings: shredded cheese, sour cream, salsa, cilantro, lime wedges

Instructions:

In a skillet over medium heat, brown the ground beef until cooked through, breaking it up with a spatula as it cooks.
In a small bowl, mix together Sriracha sauce, soy sauce, minced garlic, brown sugar, sesame oil, salt, and pepper.
Pour the Sriracha sauce mixture over the cooked ground beef in the skillet. Stir to coat the beef evenly with the sauce. Let it simmer for a few minutes until the sauce thickens slightly and coats the beef.
Warm the flour tortillas in the microwave or on a skillet.
To assemble the burritos, place a portion of cooked rice, black beans, diced tomatoes, shredded lettuce, and Sriracha beef onto each tortilla.

Top with sliced avocado and chopped green onions.
Add any optional toppings you desire, such as shredded cheese, sour cream, salsa, cilantro, or lime wedges.
Fold the sides of the tortilla over the filling, then roll it up tightly into a burrito.
Serve the Sriracha Beef Burritos immediately, and enjoy the spicy and flavorful meal!

These Sriracha Beef Burritos are packed with spicy beef, rice, beans, vegetables, and creamy avocado, making them a delicious and satisfying meal option. Feel free to customize the recipe with your favorite burrito fillings and toppings. Enjoy!

Breakfast Sausage and Hash Brown Burrito

Ingredients:

For the Breakfast Sausage and Hash Browns:

- 1 pound breakfast sausage
- 2 cups frozen hash browns, thawed
- Salt and pepper to taste

For the Burrito:

- 4 large flour tortillas
- 8 large eggs
- 1/4 cup milk (optional)
- Salt and pepper to taste
- 1 cup shredded cheddar cheese (or your favorite cheese)
- Optional toppings: salsa, sour cream, chopped green onions, diced tomatoes

Instructions:

In a skillet over medium heat, cook the breakfast sausage until it's browned and cooked through, breaking it up into smaller pieces with a spatula. Remove the cooked sausage from the skillet and set aside.
In the same skillet, add the thawed hash browns. Cook them according to the package instructions until they're golden and crispy. Season with salt and pepper to taste. Remove from the skillet and set aside.
In a bowl, whisk together the eggs, milk (if using), salt, and pepper.
Heat a large skillet over medium heat. Pour the beaten eggs into the skillet and cook, stirring occasionally, until they're scrambled and cooked to your desired consistency. Remove from heat.
Warm the flour tortillas in the microwave or on a skillet.
To assemble the burritos, divide the scrambled eggs, cooked breakfast sausage, and hash browns evenly among the tortillas.
Sprinkle shredded cheese on top of the filling.
Add any optional toppings you desire, such as salsa, sour cream, chopped green onions, or diced tomatoes.

Fold the sides of the tortilla over the filling, then roll it up tightly into a burrito. Serve the Breakfast Sausage and Hash Brown Burritos immediately, and enjoy the delicious and hearty breakfast!

These Breakfast Sausage and Hash Brown Burritos are packed with savory sausage, crispy hash browns, fluffy scrambled eggs, and melted cheese, making them a satisfying and delicious meal option. Feel free to customize the recipe with your favorite breakfast ingredients and toppings. Enjoy!

Korean BBQ Beef Burrito

Ingredients:

For the Korean BBQ Beef:

- 1 pound beef sirloin or flank steak, thinly sliced
- 1/4 cup soy sauce
- 2 tablespoons brown sugar
- 2 tablespoons sesame oil
- 2 cloves garlic, minced
- 1 tablespoon grated fresh ginger
- 2 green onions, thinly sliced
- 1 tablespoon rice vinegar
- 1 tablespoon gochujang (Korean chili paste) (optional, for heat)
- 1 tablespoon vegetable oil

For the Burrito:

- 4 large flour tortillas
- 1 cup cooked rice
- 1 cup shredded lettuce
- 1 cup shredded cabbage
- 1 cup matchstick carrots
- 1 cucumber, julienned
- 1/4 cup chopped fresh cilantro
- Optional toppings: sliced avocado, kimchi, sliced green onions, sesame seeds

Instructions:

In a bowl, combine soy sauce, brown sugar, sesame oil, minced garlic, grated ginger, sliced green onions, rice vinegar, and gochujang (if using). Mix well to make the marinade.

Place the thinly sliced beef in a shallow dish or resealable plastic bag. Pour the marinade over the beef, making sure it's well coated. Marinate in the refrigerator for at least 30 minutes, or up to 4 hours.

Heat vegetable oil in a large skillet or grill pan over medium-high heat. Remove the beef from the marinade, shaking off any excess, and cook in batches for 2-3 minutes per side, or until cooked through and caramelized. Remove from heat and set aside.

Warm the flour tortillas in the microwave or on a skillet.

To assemble the burritos, place a portion of cooked rice, shredded lettuce, shredded cabbage, matchstick carrots, julienned cucumber, and chopped fresh cilantro onto each tortilla.

Top with the cooked Korean BBQ beef.

Add any optional toppings you desire, such as sliced avocado, kimchi, sliced green onions, or sesame seeds.

Fold the sides of the tortilla over the filling, then roll it up tightly into a burrito.

Serve the Korean BBQ Beef Burritos immediately, and enjoy the delicious fusion of Korean flavors!

These Korean BBQ Beef Burritos are packed with tender and flavorful beef, crisp vegetables, and aromatic herbs, making them a delightful twist on the classic burrito. Feel free to customize the recipe with your favorite fillings and toppings. Enjoy!

Jackfruit Carnitas Burrito

Ingredients:

For the Jackfruit Carnitas:

- 2 cans (20 ounces each) young green jackfruit in brine or water, drained and rinsed
- 2 tablespoons olive oil
- 1 onion, diced
- 3 cloves garlic, minced
- 1 teaspoon ground cumin
- 1 teaspoon chili powder
- 1/2 teaspoon smoked paprika
- 1/2 teaspoon dried oregano
- Salt and pepper to taste
- 1/2 cup vegetable broth
- Juice of 1 lime

For the Burrito:

- 4 large flour tortillas
- 1 cup cooked rice
- 1 cup black beans, drained and rinsed
- 1 cup shredded lettuce
- 1 avocado, sliced
- 1/4 cup chopped fresh cilantro
- Optional toppings: salsa, diced tomatoes, sliced jalapeños, vegan sour cream

Instructions:

Shred the drained and rinsed jackfruit using your hands or a fork, removing any seeds or tough core pieces.

Heat olive oil in a large skillet over medium heat. Add diced onion and cook until softened, about 5 minutes. Add minced garlic and cook for another minute until fragrant.

Add the shredded jackfruit to the skillet with the cooked onion and garlic. Stir in ground cumin, chili powder, smoked paprika, dried oregano, salt, and pepper. Cook for about 5 minutes, stirring occasionally, until the jackfruit starts to brown.

Pour vegetable broth and lime juice over the jackfruit mixture. Stir to combine, then reduce heat to low and let it simmer for about 15-20 minutes, until the liquid has mostly evaporated and the jackfruit is tender and infused with flavor.

Warm the flour tortillas in the microwave or on a skillet.

To assemble the burritos, place a portion of cooked rice, black beans, shredded lettuce, and jackfruit carnitas onto each tortilla.

Top with sliced avocado and chopped fresh cilantro.

Add any optional toppings you desire, such as salsa, diced tomatoes, sliced jalapeños, or vegan sour cream.

Fold the sides of the tortilla over the filling, then roll it up tightly into a burrito.

Serve the Jackfruit Carnitas Burritos immediately, and enjoy the delicious and flavorful vegan meal!

These Jackfruit Carnitas Burritos are packed with savory and tender jackfruit, along with rice, beans, avocado, and fresh vegetables, making them a satisfying and delicious vegan meal option. Feel free to customize the recipe with your favorite burrito fillings and toppings. Enjoy!

Thai Peanut Chicken Burrito

Ingredients:

For the Thai Peanut Chicken:

- 1 pound boneless, skinless chicken breasts, thinly sliced
- 2 tablespoons soy sauce
- 2 tablespoons peanut butter
- 2 tablespoons lime juice
- 2 tablespoons honey
- 2 cloves garlic, minced
- 1 tablespoon grated fresh ginger
- 1 teaspoon sesame oil
- 1/2 teaspoon crushed red pepper flakes (adjust to taste)
- Salt and pepper to taste
- 1 tablespoon vegetable oil

For the Burrito:

- 4 large flour tortillas
- 1 cup cooked rice (jasmine rice works well)
- 1 cup shredded carrots
- 1 cup shredded purple cabbage
- 1/4 cup chopped fresh cilantro
- 1/4 cup chopped roasted peanuts
- Optional toppings: sliced green onions, sliced red chili peppers, lime wedges

Instructions:

In a bowl, whisk together soy sauce, peanut butter, lime juice, honey, minced garlic, grated ginger, sesame oil, crushed red pepper flakes, salt, and pepper to make the marinade.

Add the thinly sliced chicken breasts to the marinade and toss until evenly coated. Let it marinate for at least 30 minutes in the refrigerator.

Heat vegetable oil in a skillet over medium-high heat. Add the marinated chicken to the skillet and cook for 5-6 minutes, stirring occasionally, until the chicken is cooked through and nicely browned. Remove from heat and set aside.

Warm the flour tortillas in the microwave or on a skillet.

To assemble the burritos, place a portion of cooked rice, shredded carrots, shredded purple cabbage, and cooked Thai peanut chicken onto each tortilla. Sprinkle chopped fresh cilantro and chopped roasted peanuts on top of the filling.

Add any optional toppings you desire, such as sliced green onions, sliced red chili peppers, or a squeeze of lime juice.

Fold the sides of the tortilla over the filling, then roll it up tightly into a burrito. Serve the Thai Peanut Chicken Burritos immediately, and enjoy the delicious fusion of Thai flavors!

These Thai Peanut Chicken Burritos are packed with tender and flavorful chicken, crunchy vegetables, and aromatic herbs, making them a delightful twist on the classic burrito. Feel free to customize the recipe with your favorite fillings and toppings. Enjoy!

Spinach and Mushroom Breakfast Burrito

Ingredients:

For the Spinach and Mushroom Filling:

- 2 tablespoons olive oil
- 8 ounces mushrooms, sliced
- 2 cups fresh spinach leaves
- 1 small onion, diced
- 2 cloves garlic, minced
- Salt and pepper to taste

For the Burrito:

- 4 large flour tortillas
- 8 large eggs
- 1/4 cup milk (optional)
- Salt and pepper to taste
- 1 cup shredded cheddar cheese (or your favorite cheese)
- Optional toppings: salsa, avocado slices, sour cream, chopped cilantro

Instructions:

Heat olive oil in a large skillet over medium heat. Add diced onion and cook until softened, about 5 minutes. Add minced garlic and cook for another minute until fragrant.

Add sliced mushrooms to the skillet and cook until they release their moisture and become tender, about 5-7 minutes.

Add fresh spinach leaves to the skillet and cook until wilted, about 2-3 minutes. Season with salt and pepper to taste. Remove from heat and set aside.

In a bowl, whisk together eggs, milk (if using), salt, and pepper.

Heat a large skillet over medium heat. Pour the beaten eggs into the skillet and cook, stirring occasionally, until they're scrambled and cooked to your desired consistency. Remove from heat.

Warm the flour tortillas in the microwave or on a skillet.

To assemble the burritos, place a portion of scrambled eggs and spinach-mushroom filling onto each tortilla.

Sprinkle shredded cheese on top of the filling.

Add any optional toppings you desire, such as salsa, avocado slices, sour cream, or chopped cilantro.
Fold the sides of the tortilla over the filling, then roll it up tightly into a burrito.
Serve the Spinach and Mushroom Breakfast Burritos immediately, and enjoy the delicious and nutritious meal!

These Spinach and Mushroom Breakfast Burritos are packed with flavorful sautéed mushrooms, nutritious spinach, fluffy scrambled eggs, and melted cheese, making them a satisfying and delicious breakfast option. Feel free to customize the recipe with your favorite fillings and toppings. Enjoy!

Hawaiian BBQ Chicken Burrito

Ingredients:

For the Hawaiian BBQ Chicken:

- 1 pound boneless, skinless chicken breasts, diced
- 1 cup pineapple chunks (fresh or canned)
- 1/2 cup barbecue sauce
- 2 tablespoons soy sauce
- 2 cloves garlic, minced
- 1 tablespoon brown sugar
- 1 tablespoon vegetable oil
- Salt and pepper to taste

For the Burrito:

- 4 large flour tortillas
- 1 cup cooked rice
- 1 cup black beans, drained and rinsed
- 1 cup shredded Monterey Jack cheese
- 1/2 cup diced red bell pepper
- 1/4 cup chopped red onion
- 1/4 cup chopped fresh cilantro
- Optional toppings: sliced avocado, sliced green onions, lime wedges

Instructions:

In a bowl, combine barbecue sauce, soy sauce, minced garlic, brown sugar, salt, and pepper to make the marinade.

Add the diced chicken breasts to the marinade and toss until evenly coated. Let it marinate for at least 30 minutes in the refrigerator.

Heat vegetable oil in a large skillet over medium-high heat. Add the marinated chicken to the skillet and cook for 6-8 minutes, stirring occasionally, until the chicken is cooked through and caramelized. Remove from heat and set aside.

Warm the flour tortillas in the microwave or on a skillet.

To assemble the burritos, place a portion of cooked rice, black beans, shredded Monterey Jack cheese, diced red bell pepper, and chopped red onion onto each tortilla.
Add a portion of the cooked Hawaiian BBQ chicken on top of the filling.
Sprinkle chopped fresh cilantro on top.
Add any optional toppings you desire, such as sliced avocado, sliced green onions, or a squeeze of lime juice.
Fold the sides of the tortilla over the filling, then roll it up tightly into a burrito.
Serve the Hawaiian BBQ Chicken Burritos immediately, and enjoy the delicious tropical flavors!

These Hawaiian BBQ Chicken Burritos are packed with sweet and tangy chicken, rice, beans, cheese, and colorful vegetables, making them a delightful fusion of Hawaiian and Tex-Mex flavors. Feel free to customize the recipe with your favorite fillings and toppings. Enjoy!

Bacon, Egg, and Cheese Breakfast Burrito

Ingredients:

- 4 slices of bacon
- 4 large eggs
- Salt and pepper to taste
- 1 cup shredded cheddar cheese
- 4 large flour tortillas
- Optional: salsa, hot sauce, avocado, diced tomatoes, or any other desired toppings

Instructions:

Cook the bacon: In a skillet over medium heat, cook the bacon until it's crispy. Remove the bacon from the skillet and place it on a paper towel-lined plate to drain excess grease. Once cooled, chop the bacon into small pieces.

Scramble the eggs: In the same skillet, using the remaining bacon grease or a little butter or oil if needed, crack the eggs into the skillet. Season with salt and pepper to taste. Scramble the eggs until they are fully cooked but still moist. Remove from heat.

Assemble the burritos: Lay out the flour tortillas on a clean surface. Divide the scrambled eggs evenly among the tortillas, placing them in the center. Sprinkle shredded cheddar cheese on top of the eggs. Add the chopped bacon on top of the cheese.

Fold the burritos: Fold the sides of each tortilla over the filling, then fold the bottom edge up and over the filling, tucking it tightly. Roll the burrito up, ensuring it's tightly sealed.

Heat the burritos: In a clean skillet or on a griddle over medium heat, place the burritos seam-side down. Cook for 2-3 minutes on each side, or until the tortillas are golden brown and crispy, and the cheese is melted.

Serve: Once cooked, remove the burritos from the skillet and place them on a serving plate. You can serve them as is or with optional toppings such as salsa, hot sauce, avocado, diced tomatoes, or any other toppings of your choice.

Enjoy your delicious bacon, egg, and cheese breakfast burrito!

Mediterranean Falafel Burrito

Ingredients:

For the falafel:

- 1 can (15 ounces) chickpeas, drained and rinsed
- 2 cloves garlic, minced
- 1/4 cup chopped fresh parsley
- 1/4 cup chopped fresh cilantro
- 1 teaspoon ground cumin
- 1 teaspoon ground coriander
- 1/2 teaspoon salt
- 1/4 teaspoon black pepper
- 2 tablespoons all-purpose flour
- 2 tablespoons olive oil (for frying)

For the burrito:

- 4 large flour tortillas
- 1 cup cooked quinoa or rice
- 1 cup diced cucumber
- 1 cup diced tomato
- 1/2 cup crumbled feta cheese
- 1/4 cup chopped red onion
- Tzatziki sauce or hummus for spreading

Instructions:

Prepare the falafel mixture: In a food processor, combine the chickpeas, minced garlic, chopped parsley, chopped cilantro, ground cumin, ground coriander, salt, and pepper. Pulse until the mixture is well combined but still slightly chunky. Transfer the mixture to a bowl and stir in the all-purpose flour until fully incorporated.

Form the falafel patties: Divide the falafel mixture into 8 equal portions. Shape each portion into a small patty, about 1/2 inch thick.

Cook the falafel: Heat the olive oil in a skillet over medium heat. Once the oil is hot, add the falafel patties to the skillet in batches, making sure not to overcrowd

the pan. Cook for 3-4 minutes on each side, or until the falafel is golden brown and crispy. Remove from the skillet and drain on a paper towel-lined plate.
Assemble the burritos: Lay out the flour tortillas on a clean surface. Spread a layer of tzatziki sauce or hummus on each tortilla. Place a spoonful of cooked quinoa or rice in the center of each tortilla, followed by diced cucumber, diced tomato, crumbled feta cheese, chopped red onion, and 2 falafel patties.
Roll the burritos: Fold the sides of each tortilla over the filling, then fold the bottom edge up and over the filling, tucking it tightly. Roll the burrito up, ensuring it's tightly sealed.
Serve: Once rolled, you can serve the burritos immediately or wrap them in foil and store them in the refrigerator until ready to eat.

Enjoy your flavorful Mediterranean falafel burritos!

Tex-Mex Beef Burrito Bowl

Ingredients:

For the Tex-Mex Beef:

- 1 pound ground beef
- 1 tablespoon olive oil
- 1 small onion, diced
- 2 cloves garlic, minced
- 1 tablespoon chili powder
- 1 teaspoon ground cumin
- 1/2 teaspoon paprika
- Salt and pepper to taste
- 1 can (15 ounces) black beans, drained and rinsed
- 1 can (15 ounces) diced tomatoes
- 1 cup frozen corn kernels, thawed
- Optional: diced jalapeños for added heat

For the Burrito Bowl:

- Cooked rice or quinoa
- Shredded lettuce or mixed greens
- Diced tomatoes
- Diced avocado or guacamole
- Shredded cheddar cheese
- Sour cream or Greek yogurt
- Fresh cilantro, chopped
- Lime wedges

Instructions:

Cook the Tex-Mex Beef:
- Heat olive oil in a large skillet over medium heat. Add diced onion and minced garlic, sauté until softened.
- Add ground beef to the skillet and cook until browned, breaking it apart with a spoon as it cooks.
- Stir in chili powder, ground cumin, paprika, salt, and pepper, and cook for another minute until fragrant.

- Add black beans, diced tomatoes, and corn kernels to the skillet. Stir to combine.
- Simmer the mixture for 10-15 minutes, allowing the flavors to meld together and the sauce to thicken. Adjust seasoning if needed. If using diced jalapeños, add them in at this stage.

Prepare the Burrito Bowl:
- In serving bowls, layer cooked rice or quinoa as the base.
- Spoon the Tex-Mex Beef mixture over the rice or quinoa.
- Top with shredded lettuce or mixed greens, diced tomatoes, diced avocado or guacamole, shredded cheddar cheese, and a dollop of sour cream or Greek yogurt.
- Garnish with chopped fresh cilantro and serve with lime wedges on the side for squeezing over the bowl.

Enjoy:
- Mix all the ingredients in the bowl together or enjoy them layered. Serve immediately and enjoy the Tex-Mex flavors!

Feel free to customize your burrito bowl with additional toppings such as salsa, sliced olives, or pickled jalapeños according to your taste preferences.